THE PLANETS
SPACE-THEMED RECIPES

by Jane Yates

Minneapolis, Minnesota

Credits
Cover and title page, © Indigo Studio/Adobe Stock and © Maksim Denisenko/Shutterstock and © studiovin/Shutterstock and © Katerina Maksymenko/Shutterstock and © Sunlight_s/Shutterstock; Background images, sdecoret/Adobe Stock; Lifestyle Graphic/Adobe Stock; 5 top left, DestinaDesign/Shutterstock.com; 5 right middle, Christos Georghiou/Shutterstock; 6 bottom, NASA/JPL/Public Domain; 8 bottom left, NASA/JPL/Voyager-ISS/Justin Cowart/Public Domain; 8 bottom right, Sevinchalisherovna/Creative Commons; 10 bottom, NASA/JPL/Public Domain; 12 bottom, NASA/JPL-Caltech/Public Domain; 15, © dule964/Adobe Stock; 16 bottom, Moons: NASA/JPL/Galileo; Jupiter: NASA/JPL/Space Science Institute; Image data processing and layout: Kevin M. Gill/Creative Commons; 18 bottom left, NASA, ESA, Mark Showalter (SETI Institute), Lawrence A. Sromovsky (UW-Madison), Patrick M. Fry (UW-Madison), Heidi Hammel (SSI), Kathy Rages (SETI Institute)/Creative Commons; 18 bottom right, NASA/Johns Hopkins University APL/Carnegie Institution of Washington/Creative Commons; 22 top right, NASA/Public Domain; all other photos ©Austen Photography

Bearport Publishing Company Product Development Team
Publisher: Jen Jenson; Director of Product Development: Spencer Brinker; Editorial Director: Allison Juda; Editor: Cole Nelson; Editor: Tiana Tran; Production Editor: Naomi Reich; Art Director: Kim Jones; Designer: Kayla Eggert; Designer: Steve Scheluchin; Production Specialist: Owen Hamlin

Statement on Usage of Generative Artificial Intelligence
Bearport Publishing remains committed to publishing high-quality nonfiction books. Therefore, we restrict the use of generative AI to ensure accuracy of all text and visual components pertaining to a book's subject. See BearportPublishing.com for details.

Produced for Bearport Publishing by BlueAppleWorks Inc.
Managing Editor for BlueAppleWorks: Melissa McClellan
Art Director: T.J. Choleva
Photo Research: Jane Reid

Library of Congress Cataloging-in-Publication Data

Names: Yates, Jane author
Title: The planets : space-themed recipes / by Jane Yates.
Description: Minneapolis, Minnesota : Bearport Publishing Company, [2026] |
   Series: Space-licious! Out-of-this-world recipes | Includes
   bibliographical references and index.
Identifiers: LCCN 2025010117 (print) | LCCN 2025010118 (ebook) | ISBN
   9798895770337 library binding | ISBN 9798895771501 ebook
Subjects: LCSH: Cooking--Juvenile literature |
   Planets--Miscellanea--Juvenile literature | Outer
   space--Miscellanea--Juvenile literature | LCGFT: Cookbooks
Classification: LCC TX652.5 .Y3757 2026 (print) | LCC TX652.5 (ebook) |
   DDC 641.5--dc23/eng/20250319
LC record available at https://lccn.loc.gov/2025010117
LC ebook record available at https://lccn.loc.gov/2025010118

Copyright © 2026 Bearport Publishing Company. All rights reserved. No part of this publication may be reproduced in whole or in part, stored in any retrieval system, or transmitted in any form or by any means, electronic, mechanical, photocopying, recording, or otherwise, without written permission from the publisher. Bearport Publishing is a division of FlutterBee Education Group.

For more information, write to Bearport Publishing, 3500 American Blvd W, Suite 150, Bloomington, MN 55431.

CONTENTS

Space-licious! 4

Solar System Stack 6

Colorful Planet Crackers 8

Venus Bites 10

Rings of Saturn 12

Jupiter Moons 16

Planet Pops 18

Meet a Hungry Astronaut 22
Glossary 23
Index 24
Read More 24
Learn More Online 24
About the Author 24

SPACE-LICIOUS!

Let's learn about space and cooking at the same time! How would you like to try a planetary cracker or take a bite out of the rings of Saturn? With this book, you can make six delicious, out-of-this-world recipes. Let's blast off!

Measuring liquid ingredients

- Use a measuring cup with a spout. This makes it easier to pour liquids without spilling.
- Always set the measuring cup on a flat surface.
- When adding liquid, bend down so your eye is level with the measurement markers on the cup to be sure you have the right amount.

Measuring dry ingredients

- Scoop the ingredients with the correct size measuring cup or measuring spoon.
- Level off the top with the back of a butter knife or another straight edge to make sure you get the right amount every time.

Ingredients

Most of these recipes can be made with things you probably already have in your kitchen. Before you start each recipe, make sure you have all the ingredients you need. It's a good idea to set your ingredients and tools on the counter before you begin.

Microwave safety

Each microwave works a little differently, so ask an adult to help show you how to use yours. Be sure to use only dishes that are safe for the microwave, such as glass or ceramic. Never use metal or aluminum foil in the microwave. After cooking, carefully check that a dish isn't too hot before taking it out.

Allergy Alert!

Recipes that include the common allergens wheat, tree nuts, peanuts, eggs, or dairy are marked with a special symbol. Please use a safe substitute ingredient if you need to.

 Wheat   Eggs

 Dairy   Peanuts

 Tree nuts

 Always ask for an adult's help with knives and when using the oven or stove.

SOLAR SYSTEM STACK

A solar system is made up of a sun and all the objects that surround it, including planets. Our solar system has eight planets. Starting from the sun, they are Mercury, Venus, Earth, Mars, Jupiter, Saturn, Uranus, and Neptune. Make colorful fruit kebabs to stack up the sun and planets of our solar system.

Ingredients

* ¼ small watermelon
* ½ cantaloupe with seeds scraped out
* ½ honeydew melon with seeds scraped out
* Blackberries
* Blueberries
* Purple grapes
* Green grapes
* Cherries
* 1 orange, sliced into disks

Equipment

* A melon baller or spoon
* Wooden skewers

Each of the planets in our solar system travels around the sun in a large, circular path called an orbit.

1. Use a melon baller or a spoon to scoop out balls of fruit from the watermelon, cantaloupe, and honeydew.

2. Rinse the berries, grapes, and cherries. Then, remove any stems and pits from the cherries.

3. Starting with the slice of orange to represent the sun, line up the fruit. Decide which fruit will represent each planet, and arrange them in order.

4. Carefully slide the line of fruit onto the skewer, starting with the sun followed by the fruit representing Mercury. Push each piece of fruit over on the skewer to make room for the next planet in the line.

5. Make as many skewers as you can before you run out of fruit. Then, eat your healthy treat, seeing if you can name the planets as you go.

7

COLORFUL PLANET CRACKERS

Some of the planets in our solar system are known for their distinctive colors. One of the gases in Neptune's **atmosphere**, **methane**, makes the planet look blue. Mars is called the red planet because its surface has red dust on it. Try making these planet crackers with colorful toppings.

Ingredients

- ¼ cup fresh or frozen blueberries
- 1 tsp honey
- ⅔ cup cream cheese
- 12 crackers
- 2 Tbsp raspberry jam

Allergy Alert!

Equipment

- A small microwave-safe mixing bowl
- A fork
- A spoon
- 3 butter knives

Neptune takes 165 Earth years to travel around the sun!

Iron minerals in the soil on Mars get rusty, which makes the surface look red.

Neptune Crackers

1. Place the blueberries into a small microwave-safe bowl and add the honey. Heat the mixture in the microwave for 20 seconds.

2. Next, mash the blueberries and honey with a fork until well combined.

3. Add half of the cream cheese to the mashed blueberry mixture. Mix thoroughly with a spoon.

4. Using a butter knife, spread some of the blueberry mixture onto six of the crackers.

Mars Crackers

1. Using a clean butter knife, spread the remaining cream cheese onto the other six crackers.

2. Spread raspberry jam on top of the cream cheese to complete your Mars-inspired snacks.

VENUS BITES

Venus is the second planet from the sun. It is one of the four rocky inner planets, along with Mercury, Earth, and Mars. Just like Earth, some of the rocks on Venus create landforms, such as mountains and volcanoes. Make a granola bite that looks like the rocky surface of Venus!

Ingredients

- 1 cup rolled oats
- ½ cup raisins
- ½ cup chopped walnuts
- ¼ cup chocolate chips
- ¼ cup peanut butter
- ¼ cup honey

Allergy Alert!

Equipment

- A large mixing bowl
- A spoon
- A baking sheet
- Parchment paper
- A serving plate

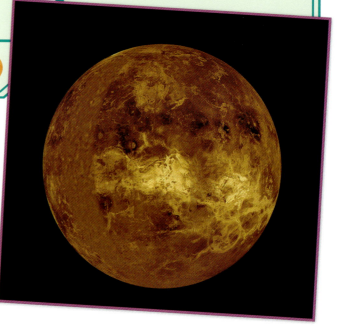

Venus and Earth are sometimes called twin planets because of their similar size. Venus, however, is closer to the sun and much too hot to support life.

1. Put the oats, raisins, walnuts, and chocolate chips into the mixing bowl. Gently stir them together using a spoon.

2. Next, add the peanut butter and honey. Mix until all the ingredients are well combined.

3. Line a baking sheet with parchment paper.

4. Scoop up a spoonful of the mixture and roll it into a ball using your hands. Place the ball on the baking sheet, and then repeat until all the mixture is used.

5. Refrigerate the baking sheet for one hour until the granola bites are fully set. Transfer the treats to a plate and enjoy your delicious Venus bites!

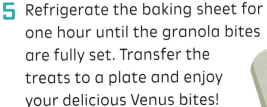

RINGS OF SATURN

Saturn is a **gas giant** planet made of mostly hydrogen and helium gases. It is surrounded by seven main rings made of rocks, dust, and ice orbiting the planet at different speeds. Try making a pizza planet with its own ring. Use cheese and spices to represent delicious bits of rock and ice!

Ingredients
* Prepared pizza dough
* Flour
* ½ cup pizza sauce
* 1 cup shredded mozzarella cheese
* 1 Tbsp dried oregano

Allergy Alert!

Equipment
* A bowl
* A butter knife
* A small plate
* A round pizza pan
* A spoon

While Saturn's rings look solid, they are actually made up of many pieces. Some are as small as a grain of sand and others are bigger than an elephant.

12

1. Place the dough in a bowl and let it **proof** according to the package instructions.

2. Turn out the dough onto a lightly **dusted** surface. Then, sprinkle flour on top of the dough as well. Ask an adult to cut the dough into two equal pieces using a butter knife.

3. Find a plate that is about 2 in. (5 cm) smaller in diameter than your pizza pan. Place the plate on top of the pizza pan to ensure the size is correct.

4. Next, remove the plate and dust it lightly with flour. Place one piece of dough on the plate and gently press and stretch it toward the edges. Continue stretching until the dough is the same size as the plate. Set aside.

5. Carefully form the other piece of dough into a long, narrow strip. Make the dough long enough to fit just inside the rim of your pizza pan. Then, press the ends together to form a ring.

6 Place the dough ring onto the pizza pan.

7 Then, take the other piece of dough off the plate and place it in the center of the pizza pan.

8 Have an adult **preheat** the oven to 425°F (215°C). Bake the dough for 10 minutes.

9 Ask an adult to carefully remove the pan from the oven. Use a spoon to spread pizza sauce evenly on the baked dough.

10 Sprinkle an even layer of shredded mozzarella cheese and oregano over the sauce. With an adult's help, bake for another 12 minutes, or until the edges are golden brown.

11 Let the pizza cool slightly before you enjoy your tasty ringed planet!

JUPITER MOONS

Jupiter is the biggest planet in our solar system. Thousands of space objects, including moons and asteroids, orbit around this gas giant. Why not make a warm chocolatey drink and use marshmallows to represent Jupiter and some of its many moons!

Ingredients

* 2 tsp unsweetened cocoa powder
* 2 tsp granulated sugar
* 1 cup milk
* 1 large marshmallow
* A handful of mini marshmallows

Allergy Alert!

Equipment

* A microwave-safe mug
* A spoon

Jupiter has at least 95 moons. The four biggest are named Io, Europa, Ganymede, and Callisto.

1. Add the cocoa and sugar to a microwave-safe mug.

2. Add a small amount of milk and stir until the ingredients are well mixed.

3. Pour the rest of the milk into the mug and stir again.

4. Microwave for 30 seconds. Stir the mixture with a spoon. Repeat heating for 10 seconds at a time, stirring in between, until the chocolate drink is as hot as you would like it. Carefully remove the mug from the microwave and stir until the drink is smooth.

5. In the middle of your chocolate, add the large marshmallow to represent Jupiter. Then, add a handful of smaller marshmallows around it. Carefully sip your moon-filled drink!

17

PLANET POPS

From Earth, the planets in our solar system all look different, but their details are lost. Scientists often use telescopes and unpiloted spacecraft to explore the planets up close. Take your own journey to cake pop planets with this delicious recipe.

Ingredients

- 1 baked vanilla cake from a boxed mix
- Sprinkles
- ½ cup vanilla icing
- A **dollop** of margarine or butter
- 2 cups white chocolate chips
- Blue food coloring

Allergy Alert!

Equipment

- A large mixing bowl
- 2 spoons
- 2 small microwave-safe bowls
- 4-in. (10-cm) lollipop sticks
- A plate
- A piece of styrofoam

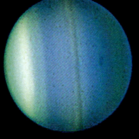

Uranus has methane in its atmosphere that makes the planet look blue.

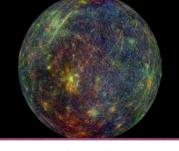

The MESSENGER spacecraft studied Mercury's rocky surface and atmosphere.

1. Break the cooled cake into a few large pieces and place them into the large mixing bowl.

2. Next, use your hands to crumble the cake into small, evenly sized pieces.

3. Add some sprinkles to the crumbs to represent the variety of materials that make up a planet.

4. Add a scoop of icing to the bowl, and use a spoon to mix the icing and crumb mixture together. Keep adding more icing, one spoonful at a time, and stirring until the mixture clumps together easily.

5 Lightly coat your hands with margarine or butter. Then, scoop out about 2 tablespoons of the mixture from the bowl and roll it into a ball. Repeat until all the mixture is used.

6 Place 1 cup of white chocolate chips in a small microwave-safe bowl. Heat the chocolate in the microwave for 30 seconds. Remove and stir with a spoon. Repeat the process, heating in 10-second **intervals** and stirring in between, until the chocolate is completely smooth. Add a couple of drops of blue food coloring and stir.

7 Dip one end of a lollipop stick into the melted blue chocolate. Push the chocolate-covered end of the stick about half way into a cake ball. Set the cake pop on a plate. Repeat with the remaining balls and then place the plate in the fridge for 5 minutes to firm up.

8 Once hardened, remove the cake pops from the fridge. Dip some of the cake pops into the melted blue chocolate to cover them. Tap the sticks against the side of the bowl to remove the excess chocolate. Push the cake pop sticks into a piece of styrofoam and leave to allow the chocolate to harden.

9 Next, add a few more drops of blue food coloring to the melted chocolate to make it a darker blue. Drizzle the darker blue over the lighter blue coating to make your cake pops look like Uranus.

10 Dip some of the uncovered cake pops into the darker blue chocolate, shake off the extra, and then add sprinkles. This will look like the rocky surface of Mercury.

11 Place the remaining, unmelted white chocolate chips in another small bowl and melt. Pour some of the white chocolate into the bowl of blue chocolate. Dip some of the uncoated cake pops into the bowl and swirl them around. This **marbling** effect will look like Earth with its cloudy covering as seen from space.

12 Use your imagination to decorate the rest of the pops and enjoy munching on your colorful planets!

MEET A HUNGRY ASTRONAUT

NASA astronaut Scott Kelly spent 340 days on the International Space Station (ISS) from 2015 through 2016. His mission was to learn how long stays in space affect the human body. Kelly says he missed fresh fruit and vegetables the most while he was on the ISS. His first meal back on Earth was a salad!

Sometimes, astronauts on the ISS get fresh fruit when a new crew arrives.

Make a Space-licious Salad

1 Put some salad greens in a small bowl.

2 Add a ball of cheese or a boiled egg to the center of the bowl to look like a planet.

3 Add cherry tomatoes around the central cheese or egg to look like moons.

4 Drizzle dressing over the salad and enjoy!

GLOSSARY

atmosphere the layers of gases that surround Earth

dollop a small amount of soft food

dusted in cooking, lightly coated with flour to prevent sticking

gas giant a planet that is made up of mostly gases

intervals spaces of time between events

marbling a swirled pattern that resembles marble

methane a gas that makes up the atmosphere around some of the planets in the solar system

NASA the National Aeronautics and Space Administration, a United States government agency responsible for space exploration

orbit a curved path objects in space take to move around planets or stars

preheat to heat in advance to a set temperature

proof to set dough aside to rest, allowing it to rise and become puffy

INDEX

atmosphere 8, 18
Earth 6–7, 10, 18, 21–22
Jupiter 6–7, 16–17
Kelly, Scott 22
Mars 6–10
Mercury 6–7, 10, 18, 21
MESSENGER spacecraft 18
microwave safety 5
moons 16–17, 22
Neptune 6–9
Saturn 4, 6–7, 12, 15
space 4, 16, 21–22
Uranus 6–7, 18, 21
Venus 6–7, 10–11

READ MORE

Betts, Bruce. *Saturn: The Ringed Planet (Exploring Our Solar System with the Planetary Society)*. Minneapolis: Lerner Publications, 2025.

Mather, Charis. *Planets: Top-Secret Data (Space Files)*. Minneapolis: Bearport Publishing, 2024.

LEARN MORE ONLINE

1. Go to **FactSurfer.com** or scan the QR code below.
2. Enter **"Planet Recipes"** into the search box.
3. Click on the cover of this book to see a list of websites.

ABOUT THE AUTHOR

Jane Yates is an avid cook who worked in restaurants while attending art school. She has written more than 20 craft books for children.